THE MAGIC KITCHEN
Second Course
2013

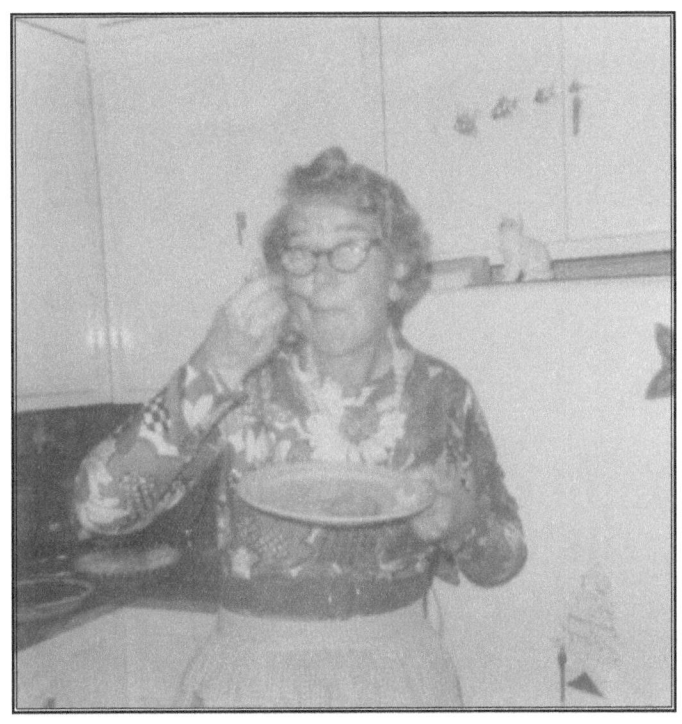

Chrismas 1972

Disclaimer
These recipes have been compiled from the magic kitchen. Success outside these walls cannot be guaranteed. No names have been changed to protect the innocent.

Contents

Appetizers

Beth's Taco Dip

8 ounce pkg cream cheese
8 ounces sour cream
2 tsp salt

Mix together and spread on large cookie sheet.
Layer salsa, lettuce, onions, black olives, tomatoes,
and shredded cheese.
Serve with tortilla chips.

Seasoned Oyster Crackers
or Snake Crackers

2 pkgs oyster crackers (cheap ones)
1 pkg hidden valley dressing mix
½ cup oil   ½ tsp garlic powder or salt
½ tsp lemon pepper   1 tsp dill weed

Mix ingredients and pour over crackers. Shake or
mix well, stir occasionally until dry.

Dave's Ceviche
(Shrimp Salsa)

Clean and peel 1 pound of shrimp. Squeeze juice from about 5 lemons. Cover shrimp with juice and let stand about 35 to 40 minutes, or until shrimp turn pink or white.

Dice: Tomatoes (about 4 cups)
       Onions (2 large)
       Chili peppers (to taste)
       Chopped cilantro
Drain most of lemon juice and add veggies and about 10 oz of tomato juice, mix everything together and serve with tortilla chips.

Jezebel

1 jar pineapple preserves (10 oz)
1 ½ tsp black pepper
1 jar apple preserves (10 oz)
1/3 cup horseradish
¼ cup dry mustard
Puree and pour over a block of cream cheese, serve with crackers. Can be refrigerated for weeks.

Hummus

1 can chic peas drained
(reserve liquid to thin if necessary)
2 cloves garlic   Squeeze of ½ lemon
2 big Tbsp tahini   Drizzle of olive oil
Puree and serve on sliced pita bread
This recipe can be adapted with pepper flakes and other seasonings or olives

Emily's Pumpkin Seeds

Separate seeds from fibers in pumpkin. Wash and toss in olive oil, dry a bit. Sprinkle with pickling salt and spread on cookie sheet. Brown in very low oven –250 degrees for about 20 min. Can use butter and sea salt.

Ruthie's Patty Shells

Shells:
Cut circles out of white bread with a glass and press into mini muffin cup pans. Bake until golden brown at 350, remove from oven and cool.

Mushroom Filling:

¼ cup butter	4 minced green onions
2 Tbsp parsley	½ lb chopped mushrooms
3 Tbsp flour	¾ cup whipping cream
¼ tsp thyme	¼ tsp red pepper
1 ½ tsp black pepper	1 tsp lemon juice

Melt butter, add onion & parsley, cook 3 min. Add mushrooms, cook 10 minutes. Sprinkle flour over mixture, stir until blended. Mixture will be very dry. Stir in cream & rest of ingredients. Reduce heat to low, cook 5 minutes until thick and bubble. Fill patty shells, top with sprinkled parmesan cheese. Bake at 350 for 10 minutes. Makes 24

Oyster filling:

¼ cup butter	4 green onions minced
2 Tbsp parsley	1 garlic clove, minced
¼ tsp thyme	¼ tsp cayenne

1 small celery stalk minced
½ small green or red pepper minced
¼ cup flour
12 oysters or 1 pint finely chopped-reserve liquor

Melt butter in skillet over med-high heat, add veggies and sauté. Stir in flour, oysters & liquor, then remaining ingredients. Simmer until thick-if too thick can thin with cream. Bake same as mushroom filling above. Liquor refers to the liquid the oysters come in and not an alcoholic beverage, although you can drink wine and make these at the same time.

4

Ellen's Easy Dip

½ cup light mayo   4 oz cream cheese
¼ c pimentos chopped   2 c shredded cheese
4 green onions chopped
Stir cream cheese and mayo together, mix in pimentos and shredded cheese and top with onion. Serve with chips or crackers

Janet's Lemon Sea Salt Kale Chips

Kale   2 tbsp olive oil
2 tbsp lemon juice   ¼ tsp sea salt

Directions: Wash and cut kale into ½" pieces, let dry. Use hands to massage olive oil, lemon juice & sea salt into kale. Bake at 350 on parchment paper lined cookie sheet for 10-15 minutes, turning halfway through. At 10 minutes, check every minute and remove the pieces that are crisp.

Crustless Spanikopita-Janet

24 oz bag fresh spinach   3 eggs well beaten
12 oz feta cheese   1 Tbsp olive oil
Chopped green onions to taste.

Directions: Line a 9 x 13 pan with parchment paper. Preheat oven to 400 degrees. Mix all ingredients together, spread in prepared pan, and bake for about 45 minutes, or until egg is set up. Cover with another sheet of parchment paper about halfway through baking to prevent it from drying out.

Apple Dip

¾ cup brown sugar   1 8 oz pkg cream cheese
Mix well–stir in 1 Tbsp vanilla, store in fridge and
serve with apple slices

Lee's Asparagus

Clean and trim asparagus. Wrap each stalk with
bacon. Place on grill and cook until done, turning
often.

Soup

Ma's Ham & Bean Soup

1 ham hock   1 lb navy beans sort & wash
1 onion chopped fine   2 Tbsp vinegar
1 Tbsp sugar
Soak navy beans in water for 6–8 hours or overnight. Place all ingredients in pot and add more water. (6–8 cups or as much soup as you want) Cook
until beans are soft.

Mary's Cheating Bean Soup

1 can (15 oz) Cannellini Beans   Chicken Broth
Chorizo sausage   Heavy Cream

In saucepan combine beans and chicken broth
(about 10 oz). Puree with hand blender, add sausage and bring to rapid boil until sausage is cooked.
Add 3–4 Tbsp of heavy cream before serving. Chorizo can be purchased or see homemade recipe in
Meat section.

Ellen's Potato Soup

4 large raw potatoes   1 small onion
2 large celery stalks (include leaves)

Boil together until tender. In large heavy pan melt
½ stick butter. Stir in 3 Tbsp flour, ½ tsp celery salt
and salt & pepper to taste. Slowly stir in 1 ½– 2
cups milk to make white sauce. Add cooked vegetables, Cube 1 cup Velveeta cheese and stir into
soup. Stir until cheese melts, do not boil. Serves 4

Mary's Potato Soup

1 pkg bacon   large onion chopped
4 cups peeled shredded or cubed potatoes
1 or 2 cans of cream of chicken soup
1 (16 oz) tub sour cream

Fry bacon and onion together. Boil potatoes until about ¾ cooked. In crock pot, mix sour cream, soup, cooked potatoes with some of the potato water(1 to 2 cups), drained bacon and onion. Fill crock pot with milk and let cook together until potatoes are done.

Ma's Oyster Stew

1 gallon whole milk   1 pint oysters (or more)
½ cup butter   ½ tsp salt and pepper
Heat milk, butter, salt and pepper to scalding. DO NOT BOIL. IN separate pan, heat oysters with liquid till edges curl–NOT BOILING. Pour oysters in milk and add 1 tsp Worcestershire sauce. Cook on low heat for 2 to 3 hours–watch closely, scorches easily.

Ruthie's Lentil Soup

1 Tbsp Olive Oil   4 chopped carrots
1 chopped onion   1 tsp ground cumin
1 can diced tomatoes   1 can vegetable broth
1 cup dried red lentils   1/8 tsp black pepper
5 oz bag of baby spinach

Heat oil on med heat, sauté carrot & onion, stir in cumin, tomatoes, broth, lentils, 2 cups water & pepper. Heat to boiling. Reduce heat and sim-mer 10minutes or until lentils are tender. Stir in chopped spinach.

Ruth's African Peanut Soup

3 tbsp oil
1 chopped onion
3 garlic cloves chopped
¼ tsp red pepper flakes
2 Tbsp grated fresh ginger root
1 can diced tomatoes (28 oz)
4 cups chicken broth
1 cup peanut butter
2 cups chopped spinach
1 lb shrimp peeled and cleaned
¼ cup chopped cilantro
¼ cup crushed roasted peanuts

Heat oil, add onion, garlic, red pepper & ginger.
Saute for 4 minutes, add tomatoes & chicken broth,
bring to boil. Add peanut butter and stir until dissolved. Add greens & simmer until wilted about 3
min) Add shrimp, simmer 5 minutes, stir in cilantro,
salt & pepper to taste. Garnish with peanuts

Mavis's Black Bean Soup

1 Pound black beans   6 cups chicken broth
4 cups water   1 ½ cups chopped onions
1 cup sliced celery   1 large carrot
2 cloves garlic minced   3 bay leaves
½ cup each green, sweet red & yellow peppers chopped
3 Tbsp olive oil   ¼ cup tomato paste
3 Tbsp minced fresh parsley
1 ½ tsp ground cumin
1 Tbsp fresh thyme minced or 1 tsp dried thyme
1 tsp pepper   ¾ tsp salt
Chopped tomato (optional)

Place beans in kettle, add water to cover by 2 inches. Bring to boil for 2 minutes. Remove from heat, cover & let stand for 1-4 hours or until beans are softened. Drain & rinse beans, discarding liquid. Return beans to pan, add broth & water. Bring to boil, reduce heat, cover & simmer for 1 hour or until beans are almost tender. In separate skillet, sauté onion, celery, carrot, peppers & garlic in oil until tender. Add tomato paste, herbs & seasonings to bean mixture. Add sauteed veggies, bring to boil. Reduce heat, cover & simmer for 1 hour or until beans are tender. Discard bay leaves. Garnish with chopped tomato if desired. Makes 3 qts.

Chelsey & Emersons
Chicken Tortilla Soup
(Chelsey makes it – Emo eats it)

3 tablespoons butter
1 teaspoon minced garlic
1 medium onion, finely chopped
2 tablespoons all-purpose flour
Three 14-ounce cans chicken broth
4 cups half-and-half
One 10.75-ounce can cream of chicken soup
1 cup prepared salsa, mild or spicy
4 boneless, skinless chicken breasts, boiled, drained and shredded
One 15-ounce can black beans, drained
One 15-ounce can kidney beans, drained
One 15-ounce can whole kernel corn, drained
2 teaspoon ground cumin
One 1.27-ounce packet fajita seasoning
One 16-ounce bag tortilla chips
8 ounces Monterey Jack, grated
8 ounces sharp Cheddar, grated
1/2 cup sour cream

Directions: Melt the butter in a large pot over medium heat. Add the garlic and the onion and saute until softened, 5 minutes. Add the flour and stir well, cooking for 1 minute more. Add the broth and the half-and-half. Stir in the cream of chicken soup, salsa, chicken, beans, corn, cumin and fajita seasoning. Continue to simmer over low heat for 15 minutes.

Crumble the tortilla chips into individual bowls and top with a ladle of soup. Sprinkle each serving with cheese and add a dollop of sour cream... serves 8.

Mavis's Sausage Kale Soup

2 strips bacon, fried & sliced   1 small onion, diced
4 c chicken broth   2-3 potatoes, dice
1 lb Italian sausage, browned   1 bunch kale
¼-1/3 cup heavy cream

Cook bacon & onion until bacon is crisp. Add chicken broth & potatoes. Simmer until potatoes are tender. Add cooked sausage & kale. Cook until kale is tender, take off heat & add cream.

Rachel's Copycat Olive Garden Zuppa Toscana Soup

Ingredients:
2 slices bacon
½ lb Italian sausage, casings removed
2 large russet potatoes, cut into 1/2 " cubes
1 med onion, chopped
2 cloves garlic, finely chopped
1 tsp Italian seasoning
¼ tsp crushed red pepper flakes
4 cups water
3 ½ cups chicken broth
½ tsp salt
4 cups chopped fresh kale or spinach
¼ tsp pepper
1 can cannellini beans drained & rinsed
1 cup half and half

Using a large 4 quart saucepan, cook bacon until crisp, drain on paper towel. Crumble bacon: set aside. In same saucepan, cook sausage over medium–high heat 6-8 minutes, stirring frequently, until no longer pink. Drain well n paper towels: set aside. In same saucepan, mix potatoes, onion, garlic, Italian seasoning, salt, pepper, pepper flakes, water and broth. Heat to boiling. Reduce heat to low; cook uncovered about 10 minutes, stirring occasionally. Stir in bacon, sausage, kale and beans. Cook 10-15 minutes, stirring occasionally, until potatoes and kale are tender. Stir in half and half; cook just until heated.

Ruth's Chicken Pot Pie Soup

2 cups chicken, cooked and diced
3 Tbsp butter   ½ yellow onion, diced
3 celery stalks diced   ¼ cup flour
1 cup fresh broccoli florets, chopped
¾ cup chicken broth   1 cup heavy cream
1 cup milk   ½ tsp pepper
½ pkg pie crust   1 tsp salt
pinch of red pepper flakes
1 cup cheddar cheese shredded

In a large pot melt butter over medium high heat.
Add onions, celery and broccoli and cook to soften
about 3–5 minutes. Sprinkle with flour and cook an
additional minute, stirring constantly. Slowly add
broth, milk, cream, pepper flakes, salt and pepper. Use a whisk to combine, then add in cooked
chicken. Heat over medium heat until warm, about
10–15 minutes.
To make crust strips, unroll thawed pie crust (for
one crust). Cut into strips and lay on parchment paper lined baking sheet. Bake in a 450 degree oven
for 6–8 minutes, until browned. Remove from oven.
To assemble, pour soup into individual bowls and
top with cheese and pieces of pie crust.

Salads

Ruth's Lettuce Salad

4 Tbsp sugar
1 tsp salt
6 tsp vinegar

2 tsp accent
1 tsp black pepper
½ cup salad oil

Mix or shake in bowl or jug.
In large salad bowl: 1 head chopped lettuce, 3 oz slivered almonds, 4 Tbsp sesame or sunflower seeds, 5 slices bacon cooked and chopped (2/3 jar bacon bits), ½ cup broken chow mien noodles. Toss and add salad dressing right before serving.

Mary's Noodle Salad

Hidden Valley Ranch buttermilk dressing made with recipe on packet (mayo & buttermilk). Broccoli & cauliflower (or whatever veggies you like) ¾ cup Sesame seeds, 1 pkg bacon cooked and chopped, 1-2 Tbsp sun dried tomatoes, 1 lg pkg of noodles cooked and drained. Mix it all together and cool.

Ma's Potato Salad

8 medium potatoes
1 large onion chopped
1/8 cup yellow mustard

6-8 eggs
mayo
1 tsp vinegar

Boil & peel potatoes and eggs and chop. Mix mayo, mustard, vinegar, salt & pepper for dressing. Fold into potato, eggs and onions. Chill before serving.

Beth's Layered Taco Salad

1 8 oz pkg cream cheese   4-5 green onions
2-3 chopped tomatoes   Sliced black olives
grated cheddar cheese
1 15-20 oz can Hormel chili (no beans)
Cream chese with milk until creamy, spread plate
with cheese, top with chili. Layer onions, shredded
cheese, olives, tomatos. Serve with tortilla chips.

Lea's Macaroni Salad

4 cups macaroni cooked & cooled
1 ½ cups cubed ham
2 cans peas drained
1 ½ cups finely chopped celery
1 ½ cups cheese (Velveeta or American-cubed small)
1 ½ cups finely chopped onion
Sauce: 2 cups miracle whip
½ cup sugar
1 tsp salt
1 Tbsp vinegar
Makes a big batch-can be cut in half

Southwest Chopped Chicken Salad

2 cups shredded chicken   4 green onions
1 green pepper   1 can black beans
2 avocados   1 can corn/1 c frozen
1 head lettuce   2 roma tomatoes
1 cup crushed tortilla chips   1/4 c chopped cilantro
Dressing:1/2 c mayo   2/3 c Greek yogurt
1 Tbsp ranch dressing powder
1 tsp taco seasoning from pkg
Mix all ingredients for dressing. Chop all salad ingredients and pour dressing over and garnish with
tortilla chips

Coleslaw Dressing Mavis

1/2 cup sugar   1/2 cup mayo
1/3 cup olive oil   1 tsp prepared mustard
1 tsp celery seeds   1Tbsp prepared horseradish
1/4 cup vinegar (cider per Grumps)
Whisk to blend. Toss mixture with 1 head shredded
cabbage and 1 medium grated carrot.

Gwen's Taco Salad

2 lbs hamburger browned
1 can kidney beans
2 small heads lettuce
1 good sized chopped onion
8 oz shredded cheddar cheese
Mix all of the above together. In separate bowl mix
1 8 oz bottle thousand island dressing and 1 large
jar taco sauce. Add dressing at last minute with
crushed Dorito taco flavor chips.

Rachel's Crunchy Asian Salad with Ramen noodles

For Dressing:

1/3 cup canola oil
3 Tbsp sugar
½ tsp pepper

1/3 cup rice vinegar
¾ tsp salt

For Salad:

1 pkg ramen noodle soup–flavor doesn't matter
1 bag coleslaw mix (shredded cabbage and carrots)
8 medium green onions, sliced (about ½ cup)
½ cup slice almonds
1 medium red bell pepper, cut into strips
2 seedless oranges, peeled, coarsely chopped
2 cups coarsely chopped fresh baby spinach leaves
In large bowl, beat dressing ingredients with wire whisk until sugar is dissolved and mixture is well blended. Break up ramen noodles in bag before opening. Throw away seasoning packet. Add noodles and all remaining salad ingredients except oranges and spinach to dressing: toss to mix well. Stir in oranges and spinach last. I have also made this without oranges and it was still good.

Caprese Salad

2 medium red tomatoes, cut into slices
2 medium yellow tomatoes, cut into slices
Sliced mozzarella cheese(the ball of cheese is best)
2 Tbsp chopped basil (can use more)
Balsamic vinegar and olive oil
Salt and pepper
Layer tomatoes and cheese in single layer, drizzle with olive oil and balsamic vinegar. Sprinkle with basil and salt and pepper. Can make several layers

Tomato Corn and Melon Summer Salad

Dressing:
½ cup extra-virgin olive oil
¼ cup red wine vinegar
2 jalapeno peppers
2 teaspoons oregano
Salt

Salad:

2 ears corn
1 bunch of radishes
1 medium red onion

2 large tomatoes
1 medium cucumber
8 oz feta cheese

To make dressing, combine olive oil, vinegar, chopped jalapeno, and oregano. Puree or whisk until mostly smooth. Season with salt, set aside.
To assemble salad start by cutting corn from ears (do not cook). In a large bowl, toss together corn chopped tomatoes, balled melon, thinely sliced radishes, cucumbers, and onion. Drizzle the dressing over the salad, toss to coat and crumble the feta on top.

Strawberry Jello Salad

2 Boxes Strawberry Jello made as directed, except use 3/4 c less water. When jello is partly set, whip with mixer and add 1 pt strawberries and whip. Seperately whip a pint of cream and gently fold with wire whip into strawberry mixture. Refrigerate until set .
Can use any combination of jello and berries

Breakfast

Grandma's Biscuits and Gravy

Brown 1 pound sausage, remove sausage from pan, leaving drippings. Add 2-3 Tbsp butter to grease if sausage is too lean. Add 1/3 cup (about) flour and mix with whisk. Add 3-4 cups milk and browned sausage, cook until thick. Add more milk if too thick. Serve over biscuits.

Tyler's Tip: Do not substitute powdered sugar for flour

Mary's Baking Powder Biscuits
(if you don't have them in the tube)

2 cups flour   3 tsp baking powder
1/2 tsp salt   1/3 cup butter
3/4 cup milk

mix dry ingrediants, cut in butter it will have course crumbs, add milk and mix into a dough ball, work it a little bit then roll dough about 1/2 inch thick, cut with a cookie cutter or glass. bake on uncreased cookie sheet about 12 min. at 450. makes about 10

Uncle Grumpy's Pancakes

1 ¼ cup flour   ½ tsp salt
1 Tbsp sugar   1 beaten egg
1 Tbsp baking powder   1 cup milk
2 Tbsp melted butter

Sift flour with salt, baking powder, and sugar. Combine egg, milk and butter. Add to dry ingredients, stirring just until flour is moistened. Batter will be lumpy. Cook on well buttered griddle. When done, yell from top of stairs "Flapjacks are done" Makes 6-8 cakes. Even better if mixed up the night before and set in fridge overnight.

Hootenanny Pancakes

Preheat oven to 300 degrees. Melt ¾ stick of butter in 9 x 13 pan.
In separate bowl mix: 6 eggs, 1 cup flour, 1 cup milk, ½ tsp salt. Pour into cake pan. Do not stir at this point. Bake 25 minutes. (Mary's note: These are horrible, but children can make them pretty much with no supervision what so ever, and they seem to like them, so they make the cookbook)

Dave's Waffles

2 ¼ cups flour (can use whole wheat)
½ tsp salt
2 tsp baking powder
1 tsp baking soda
2 Tbsp sugar
1 cup buttermilk
1 cup sour cream
3 eggs
½ cup vegetable oil
1 tsp vanilla
3 Tbsp malt ovaltine
Mix all dry ingredients in bowl. Mix wet ingredients thoroughly in different bowl. Combine & mix until smooth, cook in waffle iron.

Mary's Waffles

Buy a box at the store, toast, enjoy!

Beth's Waffles

These are better than Dave's, (and Mary's too for that matter) since the publication of Magic Kitchen he makes these

2 eggs   ¾ cup milk
¾ cup half & half   1/3 cup vegetable oil
1 1/3 cups flour   1 Tbsp baking powder
1 Tbsp sugar   1 tsp salt

Beat egg whites until stiff & set aside. In separate bowl, beat egg yolks with wire whisk until light yellow, add milk, half & half, oil, and mix well. Combine dry ingredients in large bowl, stir yolk mixture into dry ingredients, mix until smooth. Fold beaten egg whites into batter. Bake in preheated waffle maker.

Ellen's Baked Egg Soufflé

8 slices bread cubed or purchased bread cubes
8 eggs   4 cups milk
2 tsp salt   2 tsp dried mustard
1 cup cubed ham or chopped bacon
½ lb shredded cheddar cheese

Butter 9 x 13 pan, line bottom with bread, mix rest of ingredients together, except the cheese and pour over cubes. Sprinkle with cheese. Refrigerate overnight and bake in AM for 1 hour at 350 degrees.

Dutch Babies

4 eggs   1 cup milk
1 cup flour   sliced apples

Beat eggs and milk thoroughly, add flour, mix well. Pour into greased cast iron skillet. Arrange sliced apples on top. Bake at 350 until set. Serve with syrup. Can keep warm for 1-2 hours in oven.

Beth's Breakfast Hot Dish

1 pkg frozen hash browns
1 pkg bacon or sausage or both
1 dozen eggs-scrambled
1 jar cheese whiz-melt in Microwave
(Jesse uses slilced Velveeta)
Cook each ingredient separately. Layer hash browns, meat, then eggs and top with cheese in cake pan. Cover and bake at 350 for 30 min. If assembled the night before, increase cooking time to 45 minutes or until hot and bubbly. Hint: when melting cheese in microwave, stir often to keep from boiling over.

Leo's French Toast

Get a bowl mix 2 eggs, about 1/2 cup milk and 2 tsp of cinnamon. Grab white bread (Leo likes french bread or leftover hamber buns, cut off the crust) Dunk the bread in the egg mixture and cook it on the griddle. Top with melted butter and powdered sugar

Naomi's Toaster Flambe

Run from kitchen with flaming toaster in hand. Throw ignited toaster in snowbank, remove charred remains from appliance. Plug in and try again.

Janet's Pumpkin Waffles
with cinnamon maple syrup

1 cup pure maple syrup
1 cinnamon stick
1 ½ cups all-purpose flour
1 cup white whole wheat flour
1 tsp baking soda
½ tsp salt
2 cups buttermilk
1 cup canned packed pumpkin
4 eggs, beaten
1/3 cup packed brown sugar
¼ cup unsalted butter, melted

Directions: Heat waffle iron according to manufacturer's directions. In a small lidded pot over medium heat, combine maple syrup and cinnamon stick. Cook, uncovered until it steams (do not boil). Turn off heat, cover and let stand 15 minutes. If not immediately serving, transfer to an airtight container with cinnamon stick. Cool; refrigerate until ready to use. Whisk together both flours, baking soda and salt. In a separate bowl, blend buttermilk, pumpkin, eggs, brown sugar and butter. Stir dry mixture into wet mixture until smooth. Coat waffle iron with nonstick cooking spray. Cook waffle until done. If not serving immediately, cool and freeze in resealable bags in a single layer or stack with parchment paper between waffles. To serve: Toast frozen waffles and reheat syrup.

Amanda's Breakfast Special
Place pop tart in toaster. Go in living room and watch TV until kitchen is engulfed in flames.

Dave's Granola

4 cups old fashioned oats ½ cup brown sugar
¼ tsp salt 1 tsp cinnamon
¼ cup vegetable oil ¼ cup honey
1 tsp vanilla 1 Tbsp molasses
1/8 cup wheat germ
¼ cup each chopped almonds & cashews
Mix all dry ingredients in bowl. Heat all liquid ingredients in microwave, bring to boil, mix well. Pour over dry ingredients, mix thoroughly. Spread on large cookie sheet. Bake a 300 for ½ hour, stir once or twice, packing down in pan each time. Remove from oven, do not stir. Let cool. Store in air tight containers. Keeps about 1 week or in freezer 3 months.

Meat

Barbecue Hamburger
Sterling Ice Cream Social recipe

5 pounds ground beef
1 large onion
1 tsp sugar
1 can tomato soup

3 cups ketchup
1 Tbsp vinegar
1 Tbsp mustard
salt & pepper

Brown meat, onion, salt & pepper. Drain grease, mix other ingredients & simmer. This recipe tastes better with quite a bit of salt.

Salami

2 pounds ground beef
2 Tbsp Tender Quick (salt cure)
1 tsp Liquid Smoke
1 cup water
½ tsp pepper
Mix thoroughly, let stand overnight in refrigerator (12hrs). Shape in small rolls and roll tightly in aluminum foil. Bake on cookie sheet for 1 ½ hours at 350. Chill thoroughly and slice before eating.

Mexican Chorizo

1 lb ground pork
½ tsp cumin
½ tsp coriander
½ tsp cloves
¼ tsps. Black pepper
Splash of wine

1 tsp oregano
1 Tbsp paprika
3 tsp chili powder to taste)
½ tsp salt (optional)
6-8 cloves garlic

Mix everything well, let stand in fridge 24 hours.
Freezes well.

Betsy's Meatballs

1 lb ground turkey
½ tsp salt
1-2 tsp garlic
1 tsp oregano
Dash hot sauce
2/3 cup milk
1 cup bread crumbs

1 lb Italian sausage
1 diced onion
2 tsp Italian seasoning
¾ tsp red pepper flakes
2 tsp worchestershire
½ cup parmesan cheese

Heat oven to 400 degrees. Mix all ingredients and form into balls. Bake 20-25 minutes. Can substitute other meat for turkey.

Naomi's Crockpot Roast

3 lb roast
1 pkg Italian dressing mix
1 pkg Ranch dressing
1 pkg brown gravy mix
Mix powders in two cups water and pour over roast in crockpot. Cook on low for 4 hours.

Bread

Grandma's Graham Bread
(Ruth Perso Workman)

1 ½ cup graham flour   5 ½ cup white flour
1 Tbsp salt   4 -5 cups warm water
2 packages of yeast – dissolved in water

Stir dry ingredients, add yeast & water until sticky, let raise, push down, (do not knead) and put into pans. Let raise again, bake about 25 min. at 350. Mavis can make this–call her for tips.
(grandmas instructions: Stir until sticky dough – let raise – punch down– put in pans – raise – bake 2 loaves 350 degrees)

Ellie's Banana Bread

1 cup sugar   1 cup butter
2 eggs   1 cup bananas (3)
4 Tbsp sour cream   ½ tsp salt
2 cups flour   tsp soda
Nuts

Mix sugar, butter, eggs, bananas & sour cream. Add remaining. Bake at 350 for 45 min to 1 hour. Makes 2 loaves. You can sour cream by adding lemon juice or vinegar (about a tablespoon). Let it sit until it curdles

Monkey Bread

1 loaf frozen bread dough   1 cup brown sugar
½ cup butter   ¼ cup milk
Break off bite size pieces of bread dough. Roll in cinnamon and sugar mixture. Place in baking dish. Mix brown sugar, butter & milk–pour over rolls. Let raise. Bake at 350 for 30–40 minutes, until rolls are done. Turn onto plate while still hot.

Jesse's Cinnamon Rolls

3 ¼ tsp dry yeast   ¼ C warm water
Add warm water to yeast and let soak for 10 minutes. In a separate bowl mix:
½ C butter   1/3 C sugar
1 ½ tsp salt   1 C milk
1 egg
pour above mixture over the yeast and water. Slowly add in 4–5 cups of flour until dough forms into a ball. Knead and let rise for 1.5 hours. Roll out dough. Spread butter onto dough leaving about a half inch on one side without butter, sugar or cinnamon (this will help the rolls seal up). Add cinnamon and brown sugar. Roll and cut (or cut and roll). Place in baking dish (keeps well in refrigerator overnight). Bake at 350 for 15–20 minutes. Jesse has rolled cinnamon bacon into these with quite possitive results.

Frosting:
2 C powdered sugar   1 T melted butter
1 tsp vanilla   2–4 T milk or cream

Caramel Pull Aparts

2 loaves frozen bread (thawed)
1 stick butter   1/2 c brown sugar
1/2 c white sugar   1 tsp cinnamon
1 small box butterscotch pudding
3 Tbsp milk
Put thawed dough in greased pan with pecans. Pour
mixture over top. Cover with damp cloth, let sit in
refrigerator over night. Bake at 350 about 20 min.

Bessie's Pumpkin Bread

3 ½ cups flour   2 tsp baking soda
1 ½ tsp salt   1 tsp cinnamon
1 tsp nutmeg   3 cups sugar
1 cup vegetable oil   4 eggs
2/3 cup water   2 cups pumpkin
Mix all above well and until smooth. Bake at 350 for
1 hour. Makes 2 loaves or 1 bundt pan.

Yellow Bread

1 yellow cake mix   1 pkg vanilla instant pudding
2/3 cup oil   1 tsp butter extract
¾ cup water   4 eggs
Mix ingredients for 8 minutes on high speed. Pour
½ batter into 2 bread pans. Mix ½ cup sugar and 2
Tbsp cinnamon. Sprinkle over the first half of
batter, run a knife through to marbleize. Add
remaining batter. Bake at 350 for 50 minutes.

Bessie's Wheat Bread

1 1/2 cups milk
1/2 cup honey
2 tsp salt
6 tsp yeast

1 egg
6 Tbsp ground flax seed
5 cups whole wheat flour
1 Tbsp vegetable oil

Directions:
HINT: read all of these instructions first:)

I put ingredients into bread maker in order given. Oops put the oil in with the other liquids. Make a small well in top of flour and put yeast in well. I make the dough on the dough setting. I usually let it sit in the maker to raise a little longer. It also raises better if you let the milk and egg come to room temperature before you start. I take it out of the maker and split it into two loafs. Let raise and bake at 350 for about 30 minutes. I turn them halfway through because of my oven. Cool slightly in pans before turning out.
Serves: 24

Ma's Sour Cream Rolls

1 cup sour cream (not cultured)

2 Tbsp shortening	3 Tbsp Sugar
1/8 Tbsp baking soda	1 tsp salt
1 egg un beaten	3 cups flour

1 pkg dry yeast

Prepare yeast accordinmg to package directions. Set aside. Warm sour cream to warm, stir in shortening, soda, sugar and salt. Add egg, yeast, and flour. Knead and let stand for 5 minutes. Roll out and spead with butter and brown sugar. Slice into rolls. Let raise in pan for about an hour. Bake at 375. Frost with powdered sugar frostin. Can make caramel in bottom of pan with brown sugar, milk and butter for caramel rolls

Main Dishes

Bessie's Barbecue Cups

¾ pound ground beef   ½ cup BBQ sauce
1 Tbsp minced onion   2 Tbsp brown sugar
1 can refrigerator biscuits (8oz)Cheese
Brown ground beef, drain . Add other ingredients (except biscuits). Set aside. Separate biscuit dough & place one biscuit in each of 12 ungreased muffin cups. Pressing up the sides to edge of cups. Spoon meat mixture into cups. Sprinkle each with grated cheese. Bake at 400 for 10-12 minutes or until golden brown. TIP: 1/2 cup pasteurized cheese spread may be substituted for grated cheese. Cut up biscuits and put in mini pans for appetizers.

Ma's Creamed New Potatoes

Boil small potatoes or cut up larger ones-do not overcook. Drain and put back in pan. Add cream to nearly cover potatoes. Cook over low heat un-til cream thickens. Will scorch easy, stir often and watch closely. Salt and pepper to taste.

Mary's Easy Goulash

1 can chicken gumbo soup
1 can tomato soup
1 bag noodles
1 pound ground beef
Brown meat, boil noodles, puree the soups together and mix and heat together.

Bessie's Goulash

4 cups uncooked macaroni
1 qt stewed tomatoes
1 can tomato soup   1 Tbsp sugar
1 Tbsp mustard   1 Tbsp vinegar
2 pounds ground beef   onion & salt

Brown meat with salt and onion to taste. Drain
grease, set meat aside. Cook macaroni according to
pkg, drain and return to pan. Add meat and
remaining ingredients to macaroni. Heat in oven or
on stove top

Dave's Jambalaya

2 pounds hot sausage
2 cups chopped onion
2/3 cups each chopped red and green pepper
2/3 cup chopped celery
4-6 cloves minced garlic
2 cans chicken broth
 4 cups tomato
¼-1/2 tsp cayenne pepper
1/3 cup chopped parsley
2 Tbsp veg oil
¼ tsp thyme
2 cups uncooked long grain rice
salt & pepper

Heat oil, brown sausage, onions, peppers, celery, &
garlic together. Stir in tomato, cayenne pepper &
thyme. Add chicken broth, bring to boil, stir in rice.
Cover and reduce heat to low. Simmer till rice is
done. Remove from heat, stir in parsley, salt &
pepper, cover and let stand for 5 minutes

Ma's Meatballs

1 pound ground beef   milk
1 egg beaten   onion
1 cup corn flakes or crackers–crushed
1 can cream of mushroom soup
salt & pepper
Mix ground beef, onion, corn flakes, and egg.
Form into balls and roll in flour. Fry in butter until browned. Place meatballs in baking dish. Mix
cream soup and milk together for gravy and pour
over meatballs enough to nearly cover. Bake at 350
for about 1 hour.

Ellie's Pizza Hot Dish

1 pound ground beef
1 chopped onion
1 can cheddar cheese soup
1 8 oz pkg wide noodles
2 cans pizza sauce (10 oz)
1 pkg mozzarella cheese
1 can cream of mushroom soup
Brown meat and onion. Cook noodles and drain,
add soup and sauce. Mix everything together
except cheese. Bake 40 minutes, add cheese on top
to melt

Tater Tot Hot Dish

2 cans cream of mushroom soup
1 lb ground beef   Veg of choice (corn/beans)
onion   1 bag frozen tater tots
Brown meat and onion, layer in pan in following
order: meat, vegetables, soup, top with tater tots.
Bake 30–40 minutes at 350

Ellies Pork Chop Casserole

6-8 potatoes (cut up)
any vegetables
1 can cheddar cheese soup
1 can cream of mushroom soup
Butter pan, layer veg, & potatoes. Mix soups together and pour over. Place pork chops on top.
Cover and bake at 375 for 1 ½ hours. Can brown
pork chops if desired.

Ger Man's Corn Casserole

1 can whole corn   1 can cream corn
2 eggs (beaten)   1 box Jiffy corn bread mix
¼ C butter   1 C sour cream
1 T garlic powder
Mix all and bake @ 350 for 1 hour

Betsy's Veggie Burgers

1 can black beans (drained & rinsed)
½ bell pepper diced
½ onion diced
3 cloves garlic minced
1 egg
1 T chili powder
1 T Cumin
1 tsp hot sauce
½ cup bread crumbs
Blend beans in food processor. Mix in all other ingredients. Form into patties and cook in skillet on
med-high heat.

Ma's Scalloped Potatoes

Potatoes   ham or pork chops
Cream   salt & pepper
Milk

Cover the bottom of baking dish with milk, peel and slice potatoes and layer potatoes and meat (salt & pepper pork chops if using). Repeat until baking dish is ¾ full. Add cream to not quite cover top layer. Bake at 300 for at least 2 hours

Ruth's Thai Chicken Wraps

Peanut sauce:
¼ cup creamy peanut butter
¼ cup sugar
3 Tbsp water
3 Tbsp soy sauce
1 tsp minced garlic
2 Tbsp cooking oil
Heat and stir until sugar is dissolved. Set aside
12 oz cooked chicken breast
1 chopped onion
1 bag broccoli slaw (4 cups)
1 tsp fresh grated ginger
Stir fry above ingredients in 1 Tbsp cooking oil, spread peanut sauce on tortillas, add chicken mixture, roll and enjoy.

Mary's Stuffed Shells

Filling:
1 16 oz ricotta cheese
2 eggs beaten
2 cups shredded mozzarella
½ cup Parmesan cheese
1 tsp parsley
1 tsp salt & ¼ tsp pepper
Sauce:
Any Red Sauce, I use a jar of home canned stewed tomatoes, onion, garlic, sausage, black olives & mushrooms but you can use Ragu. Prepare Jumbo shells according to pkg directions, drain and fill shells with cheese mixture. Pour some sauce in bottom of 9 x 13 baking dish. place filled shells in dish. Cover with remaining sauce and sprinkle with mozzarella and parmesan cheese. Cover and bake at 350 about 30 minutes. Shells can be stuffed and frozen with no sauce to use later.

Mary's Stuffing

1 lb Italian sausage   1 chopped onion
6 stalks diced celery   1 pound mushrooms
5 cloves garlic   8 Tbsp butter
1 cup chicken broth   2 Tbsp dried sage
6 cups dried cubed bread
1 c chestnuts roasted & peeled (optional)

Brown Sausage for 4 minutes, add onion, celery and cook 5 minutes. Add chopped mushrooms, cook 5 minutes. Add garlic, cook 2-3 minutes, add butter and chicken broth and bring to boil. Remove from heat and add chestnuts(optional), sage and bread. Cover in 9 x 13 pan, Bake at 325 for 1 hour, uncover and bake another 15 min.

Sara's Stir Fry

2 Tbsp fish sauce
1 tsp shredded lemon peel
1 lg red onion halved & sliced
3 cloves garlic minced
¼ of med pineapple, peeled, cored & cut into ¼ inch pieces
1 small cucumber cubed
1-2 jalapeno peppers
12 oz chicken breasts cut in strips
2 cups brown rice

1 Tbsp lime juice
4 tsp olive oil

Sauce: Mix fish sauce, lime juice & lemon peel. Set aside. Put 2 tsp oil into lg skillet and place on med-high heat. Stir fry onion & garlic for 2 minutes, add pineapple, cucumber, and jalapenos. Stir fry 2 more minutes. Remove from skillet, add remaining oil, stir fry chicken to 2-3 minutes or until no longer pink. Return onion mixture to skillet and add sauce. Serve over rice. 4 servings.

Sara's Broccoli & Cauliflower Gratin

1 small head cauliflower
½ cup plain yogurt
1 tsp whole grain mustard
2 Tbs whole wheat bread crumbs

1 small head broccoli
1 c grated cheddar cheese
salt & pepper

Break the cauliflower and broccoli into florets and cook in lightly salted boiling water for 8-10 minutes, just until tender. Drain well and transfer to a casserole dish. Mix together the yogurt, cheese and mustard, then season with salt and pepper and spoon over the veggies. Preheat the broiler to moderately hot. Sprinkle the bread crumbs over the vegetables and broil until golden brown. Serve hot. -Serves 4

Grandma's Sweet Potatoes

Boil 5 lbs sweet potatoes approximately 3/4 done. Cool, peel and layer in baking dish. Sprinkle generously with brown sugar and butter pats between each layer. Top with sugar and butter. Bake at 350 for 1 1/2 to 2 hours–baste often.

Rachel's Turkey and Spinach Enchiladas

1 pound ground turkey
1 medium onion, chopped
Fresh spinach (I use a lot, but use however much you like–about ½ bag)
1 can chopped green chiles, undrained
1 tsp ground cumin
½ tsp garlic-pepper blend
½ cup sour cream
¾ cup shredded cheese blend
1 can enchilada sauce
8 flour tortillas

Spray 13 x 9 inch glass baking dish with cooking spray. In skillet, cook turkey and onion over medium-high heat, stirring occasionally, until turkey is no longer pink. Stir in green chiles, cumin, garlic-pepper blend, sour cream and ¼ cup of cheese. Stir in spinach last so it doesn't get too wilty. Spread about 1 tsp enchilada sauce on each tortilla, top each with about ½ cup turkey mixture, roll up tortillas, place seam sides down in baking dish. Spoon more enchilada sauce over rolled enchiladas. Sprinkle with remaining ½ cup cheese, or add more for cheesier. Spray sheet of foil with cooking spray and cover baking dish, sprayed side down. Bake 40-45 min. or until heated through. 350 degrees.

Brady's Sloppy Joes

Brown hamburger, any amount. Dump in catsup for a sauce and add yellow mustard to taste. Salt and Pepper. You can add garlic powder if you like it.

Lea's Enchiladas

3-4 cups cooked shredded chicken
enchilada sauce
Flour tortillas
1 bag shredded cheese
Mix chicken and enchilada sauce and wrap mixture in flour tortillas.
arrange in baking pan and top with enchilada sauce and cheese. Cook at 350 for 30 minutes until heated through. Then enjoy

Mavis's Foolproof Quiche

3 eggs
1 1/2 cups milk
1/2 cup bisquick
dash of pepper
1/2 cup butter melted
1/4 tsp salt
Blend ingredients a few seconds in blender to blend well. Pour into greased pyrex pie pan. Sprinkle on top 1 cup shredded swiss cheese, 1/2 cup cooked bacon or ham, cut up and finely sliced mushrooms. Press down gently with back of spoon. Bake at 350 degrees for 45 min. Let set for 10 min. to let crust form.

Emily's Orzo

Bacon or Sausage 1/4 to 1/2 lb
2 Tbsp butter
1 cup orzo
3 cups chicken broth
1/4 to 1/2 lb of Mushrooms
1 onion chopped
5-6 cloves of minced garlic
oragano, basil, rosemary, parsley, onion and garlic
powder, pepper

Brown bacon or sausage, when about halfway done add onion and garlic, when onions are mostly cooked add butter and orzo, cook for 5-10 until orzo starts to brown. Add broth, mushrooms and seasonings (we use alot, about 1 Tbsp of oragano, basil, rosemary each) cook until orzo is soft, if you cook it too hot you have to add more liquid (water or stock) *Add a quart jar of stewed tomatoes and you have a good soup. Em likes to finish it with a bit of heavy cream.

Desserts
Cakes & Bars:

Ma's Apple Bars

Crust:
2 ½ cups flour
½ tsp salt

1 cup butter
2 eggs
2 Tbsp sugar

Filling:
1 ¼ cup sugar

7 apples peeled & slice
1 tsp cinnamon

Mix crust ingredients and roll ½ of dough out for jelly roll pan. Scatter 1 ½ cups of crushed corn flakes on top of crust. Mix filling ingredients and put on top of corn flakes, cover with remaining rolled dough for top crust. Bake at 350 until apples are baked. Drizzle with powdered sugar frosting while still warm. (mix coffee or milk with powdered sugar for frosting–should be runny)

Ma's Carrot Bars

4 eggs
1 ½ cups oil
1 tsp salt
2 - 2 ½ cups flour
3 small or 2 lg jars baby food carrots

2 cups sugar
2 tsp soda
1 tsp cinnamon

Mix all ingredients and bake at 350
Frosting:
3 cups powdered sugar
6 oz cream cheese

½ cup melted butter
2 tsp vanilla

Mix in mixer till smooth and spread on bars.

Fruit Pizza

Crust:
3 cups flour   ¾ cups powdered sugar
1 ½ cups butter
Can substitute sugar cookie dough
Mix above ingredients, press into cookie sheet or 2
pizza pans. Bake for 8–10 minutes, let cool
Frosting Layer:
1 pkgs cream cheese   1 cup sugar
2 tsp vanilla
Beat until fluffy, spread on cooled crust. Slice any
variety of fruit (kiwi, banana, pear, strawberries,
etc.) Layer on top of cream cheese mixture.
Glaze:
2 cups fruit juice (light colored)
½ cup sugar
2 Tbsp cornstarch
1 tsp lemon juice
Cook glaze until thick–stir constantly. Cool, pour
over fruit–chill.

Funnel Cakes

3 eggs   2 cups milk
1/3 cup sugar   3–4 cups flour
½ tsp salt   1 tsp baking powder
Beat eggs & add milk & sugar. Sift together, ½
of the flour with salt & baking powder. Beat until
smooth, add only as much flour as needed. Drop
batter from funnel into hot vegetable oil (375
degrees) using swirling motion. Control batter with
finger. Cook 2–3 min. until golden brown. Sprinkle
with powdered sugar. Makes 2 dozen

Pumpkin Cake Roll

3 eggs
2/3 cup pumpkin
¾ cup flour
½ tsp nutmeg
½ tsp salt

1 cup sugar
1 tsp lemon juice
1 Tbsp baking powder
2 tsp cinnamon
1 tsp ginger

Beat eggs at high speed for 3-5 minutes, mix in pumpkin, sugar & lemon juice. Mix all powdered ingredients together and fold into pumpkin mixture. Spread into greased & floured 15 x 10 x 1 inch pan. Top with 1 cup finely chopped walnuts. Bake 15 minutes at 375. Turn out on towel, sprinkled with powdered sugar. Starting at narrow end roll towel and cake together. Cool

Filling:

1 cup powdered sugar
½ tsp vanilla

6 oz cream cheese
4 Tbsp soft butter

Combine ingredients, beat until smooth. Unroll cake and spread with filling, roll and chill. Slice to serve

Mock Baby Ruth Bars

2/3 cup melted butter
4 cups old fasioned oatmeal
½ tsp salt
1 tsp vanilla

1 c brown sugar
½ c white corn syrup
¼ c peanut butter

Pour melted butter over oatmeal, sugar, salt & syrup, then add peanut butter and vanilla. Stir and press mixture firmly into well greased 9 x 13 pan. Bake at 375 for 12 min. Burns easily!
Frosting: Melt 1 6 oz pkg chocolate chips and 3 oz butterscotch chips together, add 2/3 cup peanut butter and 1 cup peanuts (peanuts optional). Spread on oatmeal crust while frosting is still warm

Ruthie's O'Henry Bars

In sauce pan measure 1 cup sugar & 1 cup white corn syrup. Bring to boil and boil 1 min stirring constantly. Remove from heat, add 1 cup peanut butter, 1 tsp vanilla and beat until smooth. Add 6 cups rice crispies, stir and press into greased jelly roll pan. Melt 6 oz butterscotch chips & 6 oz chocolate chips together and spread on top.

Ellie's Rice Crispie Bars

¼ cup butter   6 cups rice crispies
4 cups mini marsh mellows or 40 large
Melt marsh mellows with butter. Pour over rice crispies, stir all together and press in greased 9 x 13 pan.

Beth's Rum Cake

1 c chopped pecans
1 pkg yellow cake mix
1 sm pkg instant vanilla pudding
4 eggs
½ c cold water
½ c vegetable oil
½ cup rum
Sprinkle chopped nuts into bottom of greased and floured 10 inch bundt pan. Combine rest of ingredients, beat 2 min. Bake at 325 for 60 min. Cool 15 min.

Glaze:
1 c sugar   ½ c butter
¼ c water
Boil 5 min stir constantly, add ½ cup rum, bring back to boil. Prick holes in cake, spoon glaze over cake and let run down sides. (don't need all the glaze for 1 cake, refrigerate for next cake)

Mavis's Delicious Chocolate Cake

2 c flour
2 c sugar
½ c cocoa
2 tsp soda
¼ tsp salt

¾ c cooking oil
1 c buttermilk
2 eggs
1 tsp vanilla
1 c boiling water

Beat ingredients together adding the boiling water last. Grease and flour 9 x 13 pan and bake at 350 for 45–50 minutes. Frost with following

Frosting:

1 c sugar
¼ c butter
1 tsp vanilla

1 cup chocolate chips
¼ c milk

Boil the sugar, butter and milk together for 1 minute. Immediately add chocolate chips and vanilla. Beat until smooth and starts to get thick.

Jesse's Brownies

4 oz unsweetened chocolate
2 C sugar
3 eggs

¾ C butter
1 C flour
1 tsp vanilla

Melt chocolate and butter in microwave for 30 seconds. Remove, stir, repeat. You may have to microwave for 10–20 more seconds, but the squares will finish melting while you are stirring. Next add in the sugar, flour, eggs, and vanilla. Bake at 350 for 30–35 minutes. Burns easily.

Chelsey's Pumpkin Pie Truffles
(Makes approx. 30 truffles)

Ingredients:
1 cup white chocolate chips
1/2 cup pumpkin puree
3/4 cup finely ground gingersnap cookies
3/4 cup graham cracker crumbs
2 Tablespoons powdered sugar
1/4 teaspoon ground cinnamon
4 ounces cream cheese, softened
For dipping: 2 cups white chocolate chips, melted
For garnish: Additional gingersnap crumbs

Directions: To make the pumpkin pie filling, melt white chocolate in microwave-safe bowl in 30-second increments until melted. Set aside and let cool slightly. Add pumpkin, gingersnap crumbs, graham cracker crumbs, powdered sugar, cinnamon and cream cheese to cooled white chocolate. Mix well until combined and smooth. Transfer the mixture to the refrigerator or freezer until it has thickened up enough to scoop and roll into balls (about 1 hour). Scoop the filling mixture and roll into 1 inch balls. Transfer to a foil-lined baking sheet. Transfer the baking sheet to the freezer and let chill until firm (about 2 hours).
When you are ready to dip the truffles, melt 2 cups of white chocolate chips in the microwave in 30-second increments or until melted. Carefully dip one ball at a time into the chocolate. Turn quickly to coat and set on lined baking sheet to set up. Sprinkle with gingersnap crumbs while the chocolate is still runny. Transfer the baking sheet to the refrigerator and chill until chocolate coating is set.

Ruth's Triple Layer Carrot Cake

Cake:

2 cups sugar
1 cup applesauce
2 cups flour
2 tsp baking soda
1 tsp cinnamon
¼ tsp cloves
3 cups raw shredded carrots
½ cup chopped pecans
½ cup raisins

½ cups oil
4 eggs
2 tsp baking powder
1 tsp salt
½ tsp allspice
2/4 tsp nutmeg

Mix sugar, oil, applesauce, and eggs together(add eggs one at a time). Mix remaining dry ingredients together in separate bowl and add to egg mixture, add carrots, nuts and raisins last, stirring to mix all. Pour into greased and floured cake pans. I use two pans and bake at 325 for 45 minutes. You can adjust pans and bake until cake begins to separate from sides of pan. Do not overbake. Cool in pans for 15 minutes. Flip out on to cooling racks and cool completely.

Frosting:

2 8 oz pkgs cream cheese
½ cup butter
4 tsp vanilla
6 cups powdered sugar

Beat until smooth and creamy. (I cut the two layers, horizontally across and make a 4 layer cake) Frost all layers and then outside of cake. Refrigerate for about 1 hour at least before serving to set frosting a bit.

Lucy's Fruit Applesauce

6 apples peeled, cored and sliced
1 tsp cinnamon
Bring pot of water to boil and cook apples for 3 min. Place in blender to puree. Add any other fruits or cooked veggies to the mix for variations. Pour into ice cube trays and freeze. Lightly microwave to thaw as needed. Lucy loves the applesauce with plums and bananas

3 - 2 - 1 Cake

In a large ziplock bag, mix one plain angel food cake mix and one regular cake mix of any flavor (only the dry powder from the boxes). Take a regular-sized coffee mug and put in 3 Tbsp of the dry mixture. Add 2 Tbsp of water and stir. Microwave on high for 1 minute and enjoy. A scoop of ice cream or whipped cream can be added to the top before serving.

Salted Caramel
Chocolate Chip Cookie Bars

2 1/8 cups flour
½ tsp salt
12 Tbsp butter, melted and cooled
½ c granulated sugar
1 cup light brown sugar
1 egg yolk
2 cups chocolate chips
10 oz caramel candy squares, unwrapped
Fleur de sel or other sea salt for sprinkling

½ tsp baking soda
1 egg

2 tsp vanilla
3 Tbsp heavy cream

Preheat oven to 325. Grease a 9 inch square pan; set aside. In a medium bowl, shisk together the flour, baking soda, and salt; set aside. Using an electric mixer, mix together the melted butter and sugars on medium speed until combined. Add the egg and egg yolk, and vanilla, mix until smooth. Slowly add the dry ingredients and mix on low, just until combined.. Stir in the chocolate chips. In a medium microwave safe bowl, combine the caramels and cream. Microwave on high until the caramels are melted, stirring every 20 seconds. This will take about 2 minutes. Press half of the cookie dough into the prepared pan, smoothing the top with a spatula. Pour the hot caramel over the cookie dough and spread into an even layer, leaving some empty space around the edges. Sprinkle the caramel with the sea salt. Drop the remaining cookie dough in spoonfuls over the caramel and gently spread the dough with a spatula until the caramel is covered. Sprinkle the bars with additional sea salt. Bake the cookie bars for 30 minutes or until the top of the bars are light golden brown and the edges start to pull away from the pan. Cool the bars on a wire rack to room temp, then refrigerate for about 30 minutes to allow the caramel layer to set

Jelly Roll

4 egg yolks
1/2 tsp vanilla
1/2 cup sugar
1/4 tsp salt

1/4 c sugar
4 egg whites
3/4 cup cake flour
1 tsp baking powder

Beat egg yolks until thick and lemon colored; gradually beat in 1/4 cups sugar ad vanilla. Set aside. Beat egg whites until almost stiff–gradually add 1/2 c sugar & beat until very stiff. Fold yolks into whites, then add sifted dry ingredients–folding in carefully. Bake in 101/2 x 15 pan at 375 12 minutes. Sprinkle towel with powdered sugar. Loosen sides of pan and turn out on towel. Remove waxed paper–quickly reroll with a fresh sheet of waxed paper and wrap in towel and cool. Unroll. remove paper and spread with jelly and roll again. Slice to serve.

Pies

Grandma Workman's Pie Crust

1/3 cup boiling water (not from microwave)
2 cups flour
2/3 cup lard
dash of salt
Melt lard in boiling water. Let cool slightly. Add flour and salt. Chill overnight

Grandma Workman's Pumpkin Pie

4 eggs
1 cup brown sugar
1 cup white sugar
1 ½ – 3 cups milk
½ tsp salt   1 tsp ginger
2 tsp cinnamon   1 tsp mutmeg
½ tsp allspice
1 large can pumpkin
Mix all ingredients together, milk last and pour into 2 unbaked pie crusts. Bake at 350 until set

Bessie's Chocolate French Silk

1 cup sugar   4 Tbsp coco
¾ cups softened butter   3 cold eggs
1 tsp vanilla
Mix sugar & cocoa together and beat in with the butter about 2 min. Beat in 1 egg at a time 2 min each. Make sure sugar is dissolved, add vanilla and pour in cooled pie crust. Cool for 3 hours and top with whipped cream.
Whipped Cream: ½ pint of cream   1 tsp vanilla
2 Tbsp powdered sugar

Bessie's Lemon Meringue Pie

Filling:
1/3 cup corn starch(rounded)
1 ½ cups water
1 ½ cups sugar
¼ tsp salt
4 egg yolks
2 Tbsp grated lemon peel
¼ cup lemon juice
2 Tbsp butter
Meringue:
4 egg whites
¼ tsp cream of tarter
½ cup sugar
Boil cornstarch, water, sugar & salt for 1 min. Stir in egg yolks, boil 1 min more or until thick. Remove from heat, stir in lemon juice, peel and butter. Pour into cool, baked pie shell. Whip egg whites and cream of tarter until foamy, gradually add sugar, beating until stiff peaks form. Spread over lemon filling, sealing to edges (otherwise it will shrink). Bake in oven 4-10 min until brown.

Ma's No Bake Cherry Cheese Pie

1 9 inch graham cracker crumb crust
1 8 oz pkg cream cheese softened
1 14 oz can sweetened condensed milk
1/3 cup lemon juice
1 tsp vanilla
In medium bowl, beat cheese until light and fluffy. Add sweetened condensed milk. Blend thoroughly. Stir in lemon juice and vanilla, pour into crust. Chill 3 hours or until set. Top with desired amount of pie filling or fruit before serving.

Bessie's Raspberry Pie

Ingredients:
    5 cups fresh raspberries
    1 cup water
    1 cup sugar
    3 Tbsp corn starch
    2 Tbsp lemon juice
    3oz cream cheese
    1 Tbsp butter
    1 Tbsp milk
    baked pie shell

Directions:
Take 2/3 cup raspberries & 2/3 cup water- simmer for 3 min. Drain and keep juice. Combine corn starch, sugar and remaining water (1/3c)- add juice and boil. Cook for 8 min or until thick. Remove from heat, add lemon juice. Beat cream cheese, butter and milk, spread in pie shell. Fill with remaining fresh raspberries. Slowly pour glaze over top. Chill.
Serves: 8

Add your own favorite recipes here

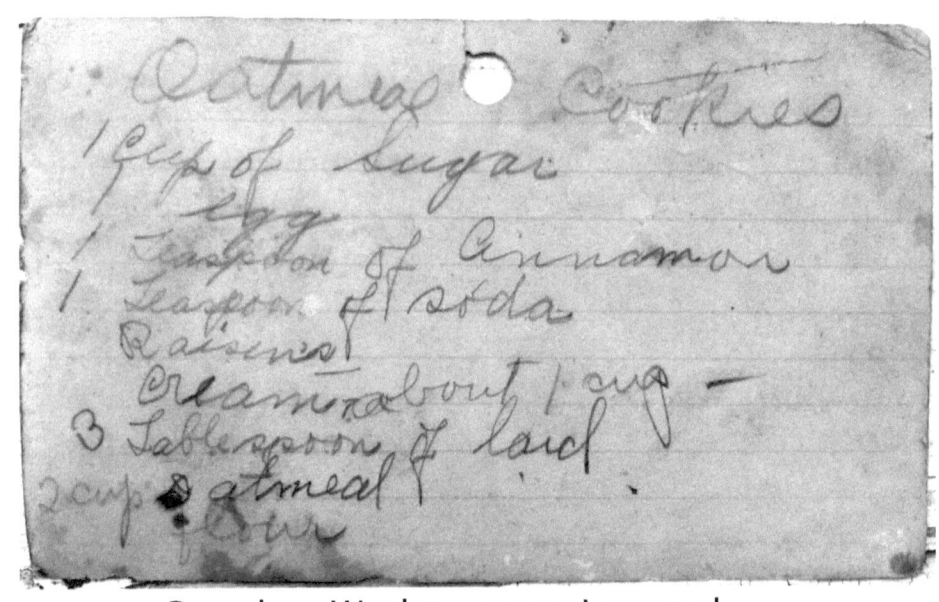

Oatmeal Cookies
1 cup of Sugar
1 egg
1 teaspoon of Cinnamon
1 teaspoon of soda
Raisins
Cream about 1 cup
3 Tablespoon of lard
2 cup oatmeal
flour

Grandma Workmans recipe card

57

Cookies

Pa's Christmas Nut Balls

1 pound butter (soft)   2 tsp vanilla
1 ¼ cups powdered sugar   4 ½ cups flour
Chopped nuts (1/2 cup or more)
Mix all ingredients, roll into balls and bake at 350
for 25 min. Roll in powdered sugar while hot.

Drop Filled Date Cookies

2 cups brown sugar   1 cup shortening
3 eggs   1 tsp soda
2 ½ cups flour   1 tsp vanilla
Pinch of salt
Filling:
1 pound dates   ½ cup water
½ cup brown sugar
Drop a little dough and then filling and top with
cookie dough. Bake at 375. (may need a little more
flour)

Frosted Cashew Drops

1 ½ cups butter   3 cups brown sugar
3 eggs   1 ½ tsp vanilla
6 cups flour   2 ¼ tsp baking powder
2 ¼ tsp baking soda   ¾ tsp salt
1 cup sour cream   3 cups cashews, chopped
Frosting:
1 cup butter   1 tsp vanilla
6 Tbsp coffee   4 cups powdered sugar

Elephant Ears

1 cake or pkg dry yeast
1 c milk
1 c sugar
2 eggs
5 cups flour

½ c warm water
½ c shortening
1 ½ tsp salt
1 tsp vanilla

Mix yeast into warm water. Let sit, meanwhile scald milk, add shortening, sugar and salt. Mix well, cool to lukewarm. Put yeast mixture and milk mixtyre into large bowl. Add eggs, well beaten and vanilla. Beat in flour (1 cup at a time) to a smooth mixture. Cover bowl and allow to raise 2 hours in a warm place. Roll out in a big sheet. Spread butter on sheet. Roll as for cinnamon rolls. Cut from roll with sharp knife. Have cinnamon sugar mixture on waxed paper then roll very very thin in cinnamon mixture. Place on cookie sheet and bake in 300 degree oven 10–12 min.

Mavis's Impossible Cookies

1 cup creamy peanut butter
1 cup white sugar

1 egg
1 tsp vanilla

Mix all together, roll into small balls and flatten with fork. Bake at 325 for 7–10 minutes. Can top with chocolate kisses. 4 doz

Gingerbread People

½ cup butter
½ cup molasses
2 ½ cup flour
1 tsp baking soda
1 tsp cinnamon
½ tsp cloves

½ cup brown sugar
1 egg
½ tsp salt
2 tsp ginger
½ tsp nutmeg

In a large mixer bowl, cream butter & sugar, bet until light. Add molasses and egg and blend well. Set aside. In a bowl, stir together rest of ingredients. Gradually add flour mixture to butter mixture, beating until just blended. Gather dough into ball and enclose in plastic wrap. Refrigerate for at least 1 hour. Preheat oven to 325. Roll out dough to ¼ inch thickness and cut into shapes. Gently transfer to greased cookie sheet. Bake until lightly browned around edges. About 10 min Cool on wire racks to decorate.

Frosting:
18 oz cream cheese
¼ cup butter
Beat until smooth

1 tsp vanilla
3 cups powdered sugar

Monster Cookies

6 eggs
2 cups white sugar
4 tsp baking soda
3 cups peanut butter
½ pound M & M's
½ pound chocolate chips

2 cups brown sugar
1 ½ tsp vanilla
1 cup butter
9 cups oatmeal

Microwave or melt peanut butter and butter until soft. Beat eggs and add sugar and rest of ingredients. Add oatmeal, chips and M & M's. Drop by spoon on cookie sheet. Bake 10–12 minutes at 350 degrees

Peanut Butter Cookies

1 cup shortening
1 cup peanut butter
2 eggs
1 tsp baking powder
¼ tsp salt

1 cup white sugar
1 cup brown sugar
3 cups Flour
1 ½ tsp baking soda

Mix shortening, sugars, eggs and peanut butter. Sift together flour, baking powder, soda and salt. Mix together. Roll into balls the size of a walnut. Place on a cookie sheet. Flatten with fork or glass dipped in sugar. Bake at 375 for 10-12 min.

Roll Out Sugar Cookies

1 cup butter (softened)
1 egg
1 tsp vanilla

1 cup sugar
2 tsp baking powder
2 ¾ cup flour

Preheat oven to 400 degrees. Cream butter, sugar, egg and vanilla, add baking powder and flour. Do not chill. Roll out and bake 6-7 min. Burns easily.

Mavis's Chocolate Chip Pudding Cookies

1 cup butter
¼ cup sugar
2 eggs
2 ¼ cup flour
1 pkg choc chips

¾ c brown sugar
1 small pkg vanilla pudding
1 tsp vanilla
1 tsp baking soda

Mix all together, drop on cookie sheet and bake 9-10 min at 375

Candy & Holiday

Ma's Caramels

1 cup sugar   ¾ cup dark corn syrup
½ cup butter   ½ cup whipping cream
½ tsp vanilla
Combine ingredients, except vanilla. Bring to a boil,
stirring constantly. Cook slowly to hard ball stage
(260 degrees). Remove from heat, add vanilla, pour
into greased 8 x8 pan, cut when cold and wrap in
waxed paper.

Yarbrough Divinity

Cook 3 cups sugar, ¾ cup white corn syrup and ¾
cup water in heavy saucepan until it forms a hard
ball when dropped into water. (almost to hard crack
stage on candy thermometer). Have whites of 3
eggs beaten stiffly. When syrup is ready, pour over
beaten egg whites a little at a time stirring
constantly. Add 1 ½ tsp vanilla and continue to bear
until it loses it's gloss and the bottom of the bowl is
cool to the touch. Add 1 or2 cups nutmeats if desired and drop by spoonfuls on wax paper.

Louise's Fudge

2 cups sugar   2 Tbsp cocoa
½ cup corn syrup   ½ cup milk
Butter size of egg
Bring to boil all but butter. Boil to soft ball stage.
Remove from heat. Add butter, cool and beat until
dull. Pour in pan

Krum Kaka

1 cup sugar
½ cup cream
1 ½ cups flour

3 eggs
½ cup butter
1 tsp vanilla

Mix and fry on Krum Kaka iron-roll into cone while hot

Lefsa

6 cups potatoes boiled and riced
1 ½ cup butter
1 ½ tsp salt
1 Tbsp sugar
2/3 cup whipping cream
3 ½ cups flour
1 Tbsp oil

Mix well. Cool overnight. Form into balls. Roll thin on lightly floured pastry cloth with lefsa rolling pin. Cook until lightly browned on lefsa iron. Cool in towels to keep moist. Can substitute 13.3 oz instant potatoes mixed as on package for potatoes.

Homemade Ice Cream

5 eggs
2 qts whole milk
2 cups sugar

1 qt cream
1 ½ tsp vanilla
¼ tsp salt

Beat eggs thoroughly until lemon colored, add sugar, salt and vanilla. Beat again. Add cream and milk. Fill freezer can ½ to 2/3 full. Use plenty of course salt while freezing

Ruth's Corn Flake Candy

1 cup butterscotch chips
2 Tbsp peanut butter
3 cups corn flakes
Melt chips and peanut butter together in microwave and fold into corn flakes. Drop on to wax paper. Work quickly

Weddle's Noodle Candy

1/2 to 2/3 bag chow mien noodles
1 bag chocolate chips
1 bag butterscotch chips
1/2 jar dry roasted peanuts

Melt chips together, add noodles and peanuts, mix, drop on wax paper. You can adjust for more crunchy stuff or more chocolate and break the noodles a bit for smaller pieces.

Party/Wedding Mints

2 oz cream cheese
½ tsp flavoring of choice
1 2/3 cup powdered sugar
Mix together. Roll balls marble size, dip mold in sugar. Press dough into mold and unmold at once on waxed paper. Makes 25
For chocolate use 3 tsp cocoa and ½ tsp vanilla
Angie's tip: DO NOT PLACE MOLD ON FOREHEAD

Baked Caramel Corn

2 cups brown sugar
½ cup white corn syrup
1 tsp vanilla
8 qts popped corn
1 cup butter
1 tsp salt
½ tsp soda

Mix brown sugar, butter, syrup & salt. Boil 5 min. Remove from heat and add vanilla & soda. Pour over popcorn. Bake 1 hour at 250 on cookie sheets. Stir after ½ hour of baking, and again at end.

Puppy Chow

½ cup butter
1 12 oz pkg chocolate chips
Powdered sugar
½ cup peanut butter
1 box crispix cereal

Melt together first 3 ingredients until thin and runny. Do not boil. Pour chocolate mixture over cereal, mix well. Pour some powdered sugar in paper sack. Add cereal mixture, add more powdered sugar and shake bag till each piece is covered in powder.

Beverages

Real Lemon Lemonade

6 ½ cups water   1 cup real lemon
1 cup sugar
Makes 2 qts

For individual serving:
¾ cup water   2 Tbsp real lemon
2 Tbsp sugar

Hot Chocolate Mix

1 8 qt box dried milk
1 pound nestle quick
1 6 oz jar powdered creamer
½ cup or more powdered sugar
Mix all ingredients well. Add a spoon or two to hot
water.

Canning
Salsa Sauce

4 qts peeled and quartered tomatoes (mash while heating)
2 cups yellow onions
2 cups green bell peppers
7 hot whole canned jalapeno peppers
1 small can medium green chilies
3 lg garlic buds (we use more)
1 cup apple cider vinegar
1 tsp salt
3 Tbsp sugar
Simmer for about 3 hours. Watch the last 40 min- scorches easily. Makes 6 pints. Seal in sterile jars while hot.

Tomato Paste

8 qts peeled tomatoes
1 ½ cup red peppers
2 bay leaves
1 Tbsp salt
1 clove garlic
Combine first 4 ingredients, cook for 1 hour. Run through sieve. Add garlic and return to cooking slowly until it rounds up on a spoon. Stir continually. About 1 ½ hours. (reduces to ¼)
Makes about 9 half pints. Freeze or process 45 min. in water bath.

Tomato Soup

2 gallons tomatoes washed, cut and peeled
1 stalk celery
1 green pepper
6 medium onions
1 ½ cup flour (a little less)
1 ½ cup sugar
¼ cup canning salt (we use less)
1 cup butter

Seasoning bag:
3 tsp celery seeds   14 whole cloves
Tie in cheesecloth bag
Grind celery, peppers & onion. Combine with tomatoes and bag. Cook 1 hour. Put mixture in sieve. Bring liquid back to boiling point and add crumbly mixture of flour, sugar, salt and butter. Stir constantly, and cook until thick. Pour into sterile jars and seal. Process in hot water bath for 20 min. Make 6–7 qts.

Nece's Whole Canned Tomatoes
submitted by Ellen

DON'T SANATIZE JARS
Blanch tomatoes in hot bath
Put 1 tsp salt and 1 tsp sugar in bottom of each quart size jar
Peel and cut tomatoes and pack in jars
Close jars and put on cookie sheet
Place in cold oven
Cook at 275 degrees for 1 hour
Shut oven off and leave door closed and go to bed– have canned whole tomatoes in the AM! (For pint jars use ½ salt and sugar)

Miscellaneous
Ma's bleach that doesn't bleach

1 gallon hot water
¼ cup bleach
½ cup powdered dishwasher detergent
Stir well, soak stained clothing and rinse with
vinegar water

Homemade Baby Wipes

1/2 roll Bounty select a size paper towels
2 c warm water
2 T Olive Oil
2 T Baby shampoo
Whisk together in a round rubbermaid container.
Put paper towel roll in container and flip upside
down for 5 min. Remove cardboard roll and pull
from middle.

Cocklebur Cure

Peanut butter
Put a generous amount of peanut butter on bur and
will slide right out of hair. Works for gum also.

Grumpy's Skunk Be Gone
(Really it's Doc Masson's not Grumpy's)

1 pint 3 % peroxide
¼ cup soda
1 Tbsp dawn dish soap
Mix all ingredients
(This is a shampoo, you do not chase the skunk with it)

Ruth's Play Clay

3 cups flour
1 ½ cups salt
1 ½ Tbsp cream of tartar
3 cups water
3 Tbsp cooking oil
Stir ingredients in large pot and cook for a couple of min. on med–high heat. Keep moving dough until no wet part is visible. Will be very stiff. Dump onto wax paper and when cool enough to handle, mush until smooth. Divide and add food color.

Brady's Camping Apples

Core apples, but don't break out the bottom. In hole left from core, pour in cinnamon/sugar or marsh mellows, or mini chips, a piece or two of caramel, or whatever you think might be good. Roll the apple completely in foil and place in coals on edge of campfire. Cook until done.

Nick's Hamburger Relish

1 jar dill pickles
1–2 chopped onion
grind pickles and onion together, add mustard to taste.

NOTE: Recipes in this cookbook have been tested in many kitchens and are pretty darn good.

www.ingramcontent.com/pod-product-compliance
Lightning Source LLC
Chambersburg PA
CBHW020353290526
45785CB00005B/2259